W9-COS-926

Celebrating Cultures

Christmas

Jill Foran

WEIGL PUBLISHERS INC.

Published by Weigl Publishers Inc.
123 South Broad Street, Box 227
Mankato, MN, 56002, USA
Web site: www.weigl.com

Library of Congress Cataloging-in-Publication Data

Foran, Jill.
  Christmas / by Jill Foran.
     v. cm. -- (Celebrating cultures)
Includes index.
Contents: Happy holidays -- The story of Christmas -- Christmases past
-- Christmas today -- Americans celebrate -- Decking the halls --
Singing and supper -- Gifts and greetings.
  ISBN 1-59036-091-5 (lib. bdg. : alk. paper)
  1. Christmas--United States--Juvenile literature. 2.
Christmas--Juvenile literature. [1. Christmas. 2. Holidays.] I. Title.
  GT4986.A1 F67 2003
  394.2663--dc21
                    2002014569

Printed in the United States of America
1 2 3 4 5 6 7 8 9 0 06 05 04 03 02

Project Coordinator Heather Kissock **Design & Layout** Bryan Pezzi
Substantive Editor Christa Bedry **Photo Researcher** Wendy Cosh

Photograph Credits

Every reasonable effort has been made to trace ownership and to obtain permission to reprint copyright material.
The publishers would be pleased to have any errors or omissions brought to their attention so that they may be
corrected in subsequent printings.

Cover: Children with snowman (MaXx Images); **Barrett & MacKay Photography Inc.:** pages 5, 15B;
Burke/Triolo Productions/FoodPix/Getty Images: page 17B; **COMSTOCK Inc.:** pages 3, 11L, 13TL, 14L, 15TL,
18, 19R; **Corbis Corporation:** pages 8, 14R (Hulton-Deutsch Collection); **Corel Corporation:** pages 4, 6, 7R,
11R, 13TR, 16, 17T, 21, 22; **Eyewire Inc.:** pages 7M, 15TR; **Glenbow Archives:** page 9 (colorized); **Heather
Kissock:** page 10R; **Courtesy of Madsen Navigation Company:** page 12B; **MaXx Images:** pages 10L, 19L;
PhotoSpin Inc.: page 7T; **Jim Steinhart of PlanetWare.com:** page 12R.

Contents

Happy Holidays

Christmas is a popular holiday.

Christmas is one of the most popular holidays in the United States. It is also an important religious celebration. Americans are filled with feelings of good will during the Christmas season. They honor many Christmas **customs**. People all across the country decorate their homes with lights and ornaments. They exchange gifts with friends and loved ones. Families share Christmas feasts.

Families decorate their Christmas trees with electric lights, strings of tinsel, and ornaments.

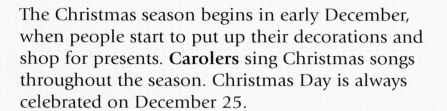

The Christmas season begins in early December, when people start to put up their decorations and shop for presents. **Carolers** sing Christmas songs throughout the season. Christmas Day is always celebrated on December 25.

Traditionally, the Christmas season ends on January 6, which is 12 days after Christmas Day.

Shopping malls sparkle with Christmas lights during the Christmas season.

The Story of Christmas

Christmas celebrates the birth of Jesus.

Christmas celebrates the birth of Jesus. **Christians** believe that Jesus is the son of God. The story of Jesus' birth is told in the Bible. It begins with a woman named Mary, who lived in a city called Nazareth. One night, an angel visited Mary and told her that she was chosen to be the mother of God's son.

It is written in the Bible that Jesus was born in a manger. A manger holds hay for animals.

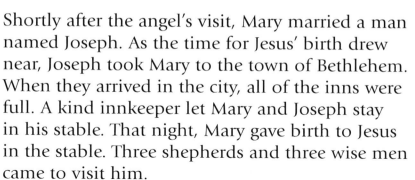

Shortly after the angel's visit, Mary married a man named Joseph. As the time for Jesus' birth drew near, Joseph took Mary to the town of Bethlehem. When they arrived in the city, all of the inns were full. A kind innkeeper let Mary and Joseph stay in his stable. That night, Mary gave birth to Jesus in the stable. Three shepherds and three wise men came to visit him.

No one knows for certain when Jesus was born. The Bible never mentions the exact date of the event.

The three wise men traveled far to find the baby Jesus.

The three wise men brought gifts for Jesus.

Christmas Past

People feasted on huge meals.

In AD 336, the leaders of the Roman Catholic Church made an important decision. They decided that Jesus' birthday would always be celebrated on December 25. This date was chosen because December was already a **festive** time of year. For many years, the Romans had held a festival called Saturnalia in December. During Saturnalia, people feasted on huge meals and exchanged gifts.

Saturnalia is named after the Roman god Saturn. Saturn is the god of the harvest.

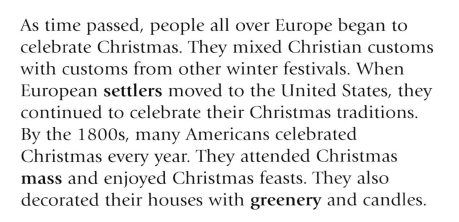

As time passed, people all over Europe began to celebrate Christmas. They mixed Christian customs with customs from other winter festivals. When European **settlers** moved to the United States, they continued to celebrate their Christmas traditions. By the 1800s, many Americans celebrated Christmas every year. They attended Christmas **mass** and enjoyed Christmas feasts. They also decorated their houses with **greenery** and candles.

The Roman Catholic Church hoped to turn festivals, such as Saturnalia, into Christian celebrations. That is why they chose December 25 to be the date of Jesus' birth.

Santa Claus first began visiting children in Europe. He began visiting the United States when the Europeans settled there.

Christmas Today

Christmas is a time for visiting loved ones.

Today, Christmas celebrations are very similar to the celebrations of the 1800s. Christmas is a time for visiting loved ones. It is also a time to enjoy music, decorations, and tasty treats. Families and friends buy presents for each other at Christmas. The gifts are wrapped in festive paper and placed under the Christmas tree. They remain untouched until they are opened on Christmas Eve or Christmas Day.

Many children receive gifts from Santa Claus on Christmas Day.

Gingerbread cookies are a delicious Christmas treat.

Children receive gifts from Santa Claus. Santa Claus visits late on Christmas Eve, and leaves presents under the tree and in stockings.

People hang stockings on the fireplace mantle for decoration and to hold presents.

Most Christian families attend church services at Christmas. Special Midnight Masses are held on Christmas Eve. These masses honor the Christian belief that Jesus was born close to midnight.

Americans Celebrate

Millions of people in the United States celebrate Christmas. Christmas festivities are held in most American towns and cities. Have a look at how some of these communities celebrate the holidays.

In Kings Canyon National Park, California, carolers gather to sing at the base of "the Nation's Christmas Tree."

In San Antonio, Texas, thousands of people take part in Los Posados. This is a Spanish **pageant** in which people act out the night of Jesus' birth.

On the island of Honolulu, Hawai'i, the Christmas Tree Ship brings Christmas trees for people on the island.

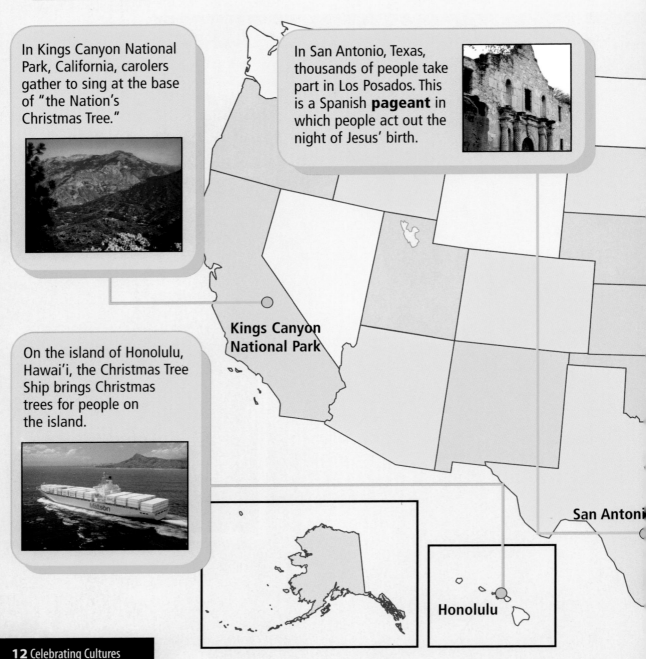

Kings Canyon National Park

San Antoni

Honolulu

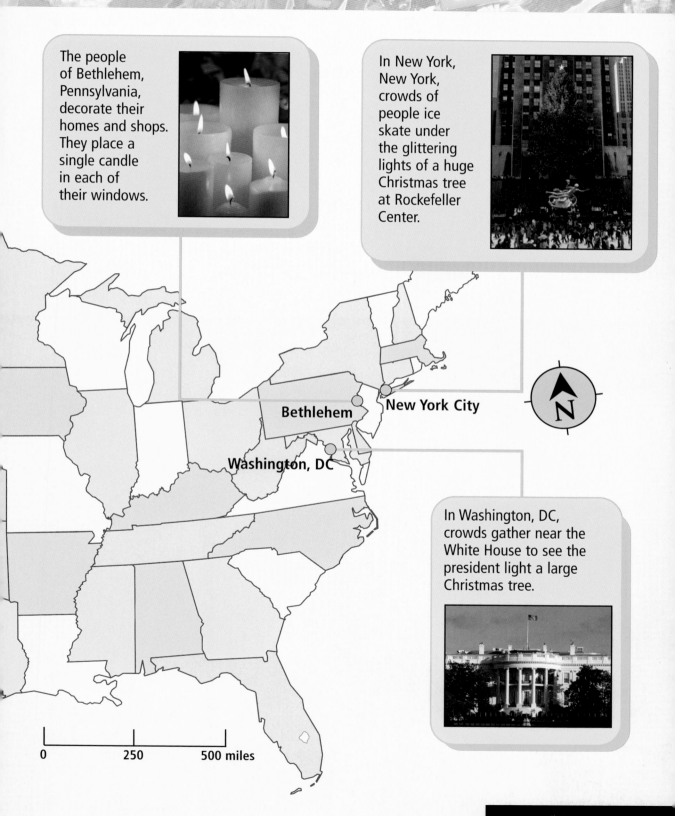

The people of Bethlehem, Pennsylvania, decorate their homes and shops. They place a single candle in each of their windows.

In New York, New York, crowds of people ice skate under the glittering lights of a huge Christmas tree at Rockefeller Center.

Bethlehem

New York City

N

Washington, DC

In Washington, DC, crowds gather near the White House to see the president light a large Christmas tree.

0   250   500 miles

Decking the Halls

The custom of decorating Christmas trees began in the early 1600s.

Oh, Christmas Tree!

The Christmas tree is a popular **symbol** of Christmas. The custom of decorating Christmas trees began in the early 1600s. One Christmas night, a German man named Martin Luther noticed how lovely the **evergreens** looked in the starlight. He cut down a small tree, took it home, and decorated it with candles. Soon, Christmas trees were popular all over Germany. German settlers brought the custom to the United States in the 1700s.

Decorating the Christmas tree has been a Christmas tradition for a very long time.

Martin Luther was a religious man who lived in the late 1500s and early 1600s.

Lights and Ornaments

People love to decorate their homes during the Christmas season. They hang Christmas wreaths on their front doors. They trim their Christmas trees with special ornaments, tinsel, and **garlands**. Colorful lights brighten trees, streets, homes, and stores. The lights help to bring cheer and warmth to the holidays.

Mistletoe is an ancient symbol for peace and joy. At Christmas, this plant is hung from the ceiling. Kissing under the mistletoe is a sign of friendship.

Christmas morning is the time for opening presents.

Many people try to decorate their homes in creative ways, using lights and ornaments.

Songs and Supper

Christmas songs are called carols.

Songs of Joy

During the Christmas season, Christmas music can be heard almost everywhere. These special songs help people enjoy the holiday season. Christmas songs of praise and joy are called carols. Most carols describe the events of Jesus' birth. Some carols have been sung for hundreds of years.

The story of Jesus' birth is often performed at Christmas church services.

A Time for Feasting

Everyone looks forward to the delicious foods served at Christmastime. Many people bake special treats for their friends and neighbors. Some of the best Christmas treats include shortbread cookies, fruitcakes, and **mince pies**. Most families gather together for a huge meal on Christmas Day or Christmas Eve. Traditional Christmas feasts usually include roasted turkey with stuffing, cranberry sauce, mashed potatoes, and rich desserts.

The candy cane is shaped like a shepherd's **crook**. The candy cane represents the shepherds who first went to see the baby Jesus.

Christmas is a time for families to gather together.

Gifts and Greetings

Santa Claus stops at every house.

Santa Claus

Children all over the United States eagerly await a visit from Santa Claus on Christmas Eve. Santa Claus is believed to visit homes long after everyone goes to sleep. He flies through the sky in a sleigh that is pulled by eight reindeer. Santa Claus stops at every house, leaving gifts for children who have been good.

Santa Claus also visits shopping malls and community centers during the Christmas season.

Seasons Greetings

Sending greeting cards is a Christmas custom. The custom of sending Christmas cards has been popular in the United States since the late 1800s. Today, people send Christmas cards to their friends, family, and relatives all over the world.

Poinsettias are the most well-known Christmas plants. These star-shaped plants are used as decorations inside homes and other buildings.

Sending Christmas cards is a way for people to keep in touch with each other.

For More Information

Many books and Web sites help explain the history and traditions of Christmas. To learn more about Christmas, you can borrow books from a library or search the Internet.

Books

Read the following books to learn more about the Christmas season.

Barth, Edna. *Holly, Reindeer, and Colored Lights: The Story of the Christmas Symbols*. Boston: Clarion Books, 2000.

Boase, Petra. *Fun at Christmas*. Bath: Southwater Publishing, 2000.

Web Sites

To get the answers to all kinds of Christmas questions, visit **How Christmas Works** at: www.howstuffworks.com/christmas.htm

Enter the search words "Christmas" or "carols" into an online encyclopedia, such as **Encarta**: www.encarta.com

Imagine if...

Imagine that your class is going to throw a Christmas party. Your teacher decides to invite a special guest. This guest is from far away and knows very little about Christmas. You and your friends must show the guest how Christmas is celebrated in the United States. What would you have at the party to help teach your guest about Christmas? Would you have a tree and Christmas lights? Would you bring Christmas treats and gifts? Write a story or draw a picture that explains how you would introduce Christmas to your guest.

What You Have Learned

1 Christmas is an important Christian holiday. It celebrates the birth of Jesus.

2 Christians around the world believe that Jesus is the son of God.

3 Many ancient winter festivals, including Saturnalia, have influenced Christmas traditions.

4 The idea of the Christmas tree originated in Germany. German settlers brought this custom to the United States in the 1700s.

5 Many different cultural groups have brought their own Christmas traditions to the United States.

6 Most Christmas carols describe the events of Jesus' birth.

More Facts to Know

- Today, every state in the country grows trees especially for Christmas. These trees are grown on special farms.

- One of the most well-known Christmas carols is called "Silent Night." It was written in 1818. Today, "Silent Night" is sung in more than 180 languages.

- Exchanging Christmas gifts was not common in the United States until the late 1800s.

- "The Nutcracker" is a holiday fairy tale about a young girl named Clara and her favorite Christmas toy. The story is now a popular ballet that is performed during the Christmas season.

- Santa Claus is sometimes called Saint Nicholas. Saint Nicholas was a kind man who lived during the fourth century. When he died, Saint Nicholas became the **patron saint** of children.

Words to Know

carolers: people who sing Christmas carols

Christians: people who believe in Jesus

crook: a stick that is bent or curved on one end

customs: ways of acting that have become habit

evergreens: trees that stay green throughout the year

festive: joyous; merry

garlands: wreaths or strings of decorations

greenery: green plants that are used for decoration

mass: a type of church service

mince pies: special holiday pies filled with fruit, nuts, raisins, and sometimes meat

pageant: a play

patron saint: the protector of a certain group of people

settlers: people who moved to a new country to live

symbol: something that represents something else

Index